Unlimited Customers

How to Set Up and Run Your Own Successful Affiliate Program

Chris Lutz

DEDICATION

I dedicate this book to my Mom and Dad.

Contents

ACKNOWLEDGMENTS

Special thanks to Rachel Wright for teaching me all she knows about business on the web.

Introduction

Good old affiliate promotion, the lifeblood of many businesses: underestimated or ignored by many more. In this manual, I want to take you on a journey through the inner workings of a well-oiled affiliate program. We'll talk about everything from the importance of running such a system, through to getting affiliates promoting when you want them to, and some stats for you to have a look at that will squash any doubt that this is one of the most profitable aspects of online business, and I'll make sure to get at least one interactive quiz in there to make things a more interesting read, and to test your knowledge.

Even if you don't have an affiliate program set up for your own business yet, give it a shot. Skim over it at least. It's not hard to understand or set up once you have the facts, not to mention the mighty profit potential it puts at your disposal.

So, grab a cup of your favorite drink, sink into your most comfortable chair, and let's get started.

Overview of Affiliate Management

● To give you up front knowledge about how to effectively and profitably maintain your business' affiliate system before the first affiliate even lands on your doorstep.

● To demonstrate how powerful affiliate marketing is, and why no marketer should be without it.

● To look at some figures of product sales and profit both with and without affiliate programs functioning. How effective is this? You decide.

● To open your mind when it comes to setting your commissions and understand the concept of reaping resources being far more powerful than any small percentage you can keep from your affiliates.

● To discuss the inner workings of affiliate sales through commission level setting for your business, taking into account the money making power you're going to build for yourself.

● To show you how to overcome the problem of affiliates not promoting your products for you.

Effective Affiliate Program Management

Welcome to effective affiliate program management. I wrote this for one reason, and one reason only, and that's to show you how to maintain both your affiliate system, the affiliates contained within it, the offers you send them, and how to get the most out of all of the above. Also, I'll be talking to you about what not do to with them, why they're so important and some of the reasons that affiliates and affiliate systems are often underestimated or seen in a negative light from the perspective of program owners looking solely at their short to medium term profit.

One thing I will say is that It's important to acquire and consume this knowledge at the earliest stage possible for reasons we'll discuss shortly. Even it isn't your top priority at this particular moment, you'll be able to see just how powerful affiliate marketing is and why you should start planning before even launching your products.

What You Won't Find Here

What you won't find here is any technical talk on how to install scripts, which scripts to use, coding, how to make them look pretty or anything like that, because if you haven't already guessed, we're a purely practical marketing theory based guide (proven and tested theory that is), and not a techy guide, or a dressed up marketing guide that overlaps into these categories to make the manual look bigger.

Setting the Scene - Displaying the Power

Lets take it from the top. First up, how do you define an affiliate program, or affiliate system? A system in which an owner or licensee of a product allows people outside of his or her own company to promote for them for a percentage of the commissions.

Pretty much everyone online uses this resource to their advantage, because lets face it, it's far easier for 100 people to sell 1000 units of a product than it is to have one person sell a thousand units of a product. I'm sure it's possible, but we don't have all the time in the world, so affiliates are generally the answer, and should make up a large amount of your business' revenue if you're promoting your own products.

In case you're kind of underestimating the situation, don't have any affiliate system in place, or haven't decided to fully utilize this type of system within your business, let me put a scene to you to make this all crystal clear. Here's the situation;

You're a business owner, you've just launched your shiny new site, which just happens to sell the same product as Mr. X here. Both yours and Mr. X's product is priced at $500. The difference is you've built yourself up a relatively modest 150 affiliates, and Mr. X is doing all the promotion alone.

Now imagine you each make ten sales in the first month through personal promotion. You both make $5000. Great, but when your affiliates come in, it's easy to see how this figure can double. Now of course not all of your affiliates are going to be heavy hitters, great promoters or even make any sales at all, ever. But lets say just 10% of your affiliates, just 15 of them, make a measly three sales each in that same month at 60% commissions, which I'll set higher than average right now for a reason I'll reveal in a moment.

Pulling out my handy calculator, I can tell you that through those three sales from a small percentage of your affiliates, you've just made an extra $9000, bringing your total to $14000 for that month. You're laughing, and poor Mr. X. He was one of the many marketers out there that didn't take this type of affiliate marketing seriously, or d dn't see any real profit in it. Meanwhile, you've just pocketed in a month what it takes most of my friends in regular jobs to earn in four or five months, often longer. Cool huh?

Why Don't You Set It Up?

So now you can see how important this is, never ever let anyone tell you it's not worth spending the extra money on the set up of an affiliate program, made even easier nowadays by the plethora of software and solutions available to you as an online business owner.

"So why not set one up? They're more than doubling my income", I used to say to my less experienced contacts in the online business world. Ask yours the same question if you like and see what they say. The reasons they'll give you when you ask why they hold their negative opinion on this subject, more often than not will be that in their experience hardly any of their affiliates promote. Well, they're not wrong, it varies from business to business, but many affiliates don't bother to promote, or sign up meaning to and forget, or just don't have their resources built to a point where they have the promotion power to make the sales. This doesn't mean that you shouldn't still grab them at every opportunity, as you can see here from just that small example above, just 10% of affiliates promoting, making a small (very small) amount of sales each can easily double, triple., quadruple your income and sometimes even more. Looking at these figures always gets me excited. Have you ever seen someone making 40-50, 60 or 100 thousand dollars a month and wondered to yourself how the heck they pull that kind of cash out of their products when you're struggling to hit five or ten thousand a month? Well let me tell you, this is a very big part of it. Don't miss out, or you might find yourself just getting by instead of extremely comfortable where income is concerned.

The second reason you might be told that having affiliates promote for you is a waste of time and effort on your part, is that they're hard to find. It's another one of those little niggly things, like the list craze going on all around us. In general the more responsive your list, the more cash you're going to make out of them now and in the future. This is exactly the same. Don't ever let anyone tell you that you're making a mistake putting a successful affiliate program high on your list of priorities, even over making direct sales.

So What Makes Your Situation Any Different?

What we're going to look at now is what to do with your affiliates to try and hit and exceed that ten percent promotion rate. Once again, if you're not sure about getting the affiliates in the first place and maintaining them doesn't interest you right now, not to worry. The moment you begin to build your list and launch products all of this will become relevant.

Continuing with management of affiliates, you might be surprised to find out it's not all that complicated and relates closely to other forms of resource gathering, from lists, to customers, joint ventures and the like.

You're Making Money, Not Losing It Dashing the Affiliate Doubts

We're going to jump ahead now, and start to build up a picture of the ideal affiliate program, with a view to getting your affiliates promoting. The rest of this report contains some fundamentals, so keep reading along with us even if you don't have a system set up yet, because it will provide solid knowledge base and assist you in understanding what your software needs to be capable of.

So where do we start with affiliate marketing? Well, the first and most important thing I want to get out of your mind is that you're losing money, or the amount of money you gain by putting in the extra time and effort to run an affiliate program isn't worth it. I want to show you a few more examples and sum it up with a couple of sentences that should dash any doubts you have in your mind about whether this is all worth it or not.

Let's look at a different example this time, one where the price and short term gains aren't quite so visible. Take a membership site. Let's say you're running it at a modest $15 per month. I could sit here and tell you that with 200 members that you referred yourself is $3000 per month. Not bad. A handy little earner there. The problem comes when you start talking about giving 60% commissions to affiliates who promote for you. It doesn't seem like a good deal at all. That leaves you with a rather tiny $6 profit per sale per month.

I think this is where the whole affiliate program is a bad deal state of mind comes up a lot with the people I meet. That looks like a massive cut in profits, but let's say again that you have 150 affiliates, and this time, due to the lower price, and it being slightly easier to get people to part with their cash compared to a $500 product, 15 of your affiliates refer 15 members each that just happen to stay with you for a year. That's a minuscule $337.50 extra per week. Now some might see that as not worth it, but let's add that up. $1350 per month, or $16,200 per year. Looks a little better now. I could buy myself a 64" plasma screen with that, or 6 brand new top of the range computers. What would you buy with an extra $16k a year? Not a bad little earner for something that originally took your profit per sale down to a hardly impressive $6.

So here's the thing, and this applies to all cases I can think of. If it's viable to have an affiliate program, have one, because lets face it; a sale by an affiliate that cuts your profits on that sale by 60% isn't a 60% loss, it's a 40% gain on a sale that quite likely would not have been made without that affiliate. The potential for this is huge, but we're done with examples for now. If that didn't persuade you that having a solid line of affiliates ready to promote for you is as important, if not more important than having your own list, nothing will.

Look at it this way. With affiliate marketing you're kind of adding to the resources you have on hand, and your promotion power. As much as joint ventures and a big hungry and responsive mailing list are great, they're massively enhanced by a few hundred affiliates going for you.

Ok, it's time to look at management of your affiliates themselves, how to get them to promote in the most profitable way possible depending on your product.

Not an Overnight Task

Doesn't Mean It Can't Be Fast

Ok, let's get started. The first thing I want at the front of your mind when going through this is affiliate sales and affiliate building is not an overnight thing. I could lie to you, but I won't. Affiliate building is like list building. The more products you create and promote, the more affiliates are likely to join you on the way. Like with list building, the more joint ventures and promotions you get sorted, the more people will join your list on the way. Understand that if this is your first day, and you don't have any affiliates they will only grow as fast as you promote. Keep in mind though, that even five good new affiliates wil put you well on your way to earning a heck of a lot more.

Your First Questions

In setting up your affiliate program, the first question you'll likely have to ask yourself is how much do I award to affiliates per sale and on how many levels? While there are many factors to take into account, the answer isn't really all that complex. **Always look at things from an affiliates point of view.** We've really been spoiled by commissions as of late, I've seen things up to 80%, and even 100% for the first month quick start bonuses. This is why it's important that your first level is at least 40%. Remember that's not a 60% loss, it's a 40% gain from a sale you may never have made. If there's one thing I'd like you to keep in mind at this point, it's that when getting started, affiliate promotion is more about resource building for future promotion than making immediate profit, something the big earners realized early on. Sure you'd give away 80-100% if it meant you'd have a list of several thousand to promote to as a result of the increased affiliate activity. **Don't think in two dimensions,** or you'll see your highly contested for affiliates go elsewhere for higher commissions.

Next up comes level two. It's really important to have a level two commission going, because this will give all the first level referrers a passive income (cliché, I know) once they've exhausted their first level promotion. I know some people who won't even promote products unless they have a second level commission there (very big tip, don't forget this widespread factor), or the first level commission is particularly high. So a second level is a must, unless you have a very high ticket product to start with. Use your discretion, and remember to test whilst your selecting your levels and whilst your affiliates promote for you.

Now I understand that there may be circumstances where 40% commissions or a second level commission may not be possible. For example, if the products that you're creating are tangible, or have a high production cost, but still go ahead and create yourself an affiliate program, whether it's five or ten percent. It won't get you as much interest as a high commission program, but you really don't have much choice when paying a 40% commission rate would put you at a loss every sale.

Taking into Account the Price of Your Products

The next thing you'll want to look at when trying to set your affiliate commissions is the price of your product itself, and its structure. It's far easier to get people to promote for you in four situations.

1. Where you have a high price
2. When your commissions are higher
3. When you have a second level
4. Where the commission is re-occurring over time

If your affiliate program doesn't meet at least one of those requirements, we have a problem on our hands. The more of these four points it meets, the stronger is your position both for attracting affiliates and keeping them promoting.

Analyze Your Offer Objectively

I've had people ask me why they're having trouble getting affiliates to promote for them, and more often than not, they're trying to get people to promote a one off sale $10 product, or something similar. Now if that's not re-occurring, and has no follow-up product, then what good is a $5 one off commission for the promoter? Not a lot. Of course I'm not saying you wouldn't get any affiliates in this situation, but it may be harder than you expect to attract. The competition for joint ventures, lists, and affiliates right now is as harsh and as cut throat as the competition for actual sales of products.

So before you actually decide to shell out on some sort of affiliate software, make sure that you don't offer commissions that are too low, non-reoccurring, or don't have a second level.

Put yourself in the affiliates' shoes. Remember, they don't care about your profits. They care about theirs.

If you were them, would you promote your product? Would it be profitable for you? Would it even be worth your time? These are the things to think about when not only setting commissions, but deciding whether or not it's even worth having an affiliate program up there for people to take advantage of in the first place. If you can't answer those two questions with a confident 'yes' then your setup probably needs to be changed in some way until you can, because it's likely others will have the same reaction as you, and your tracking and testing results will tell you the same.

If you don't have an affiliate system up and running already, and have just skimmed through this so far, I would suggest coming back and using this as a reference when you do start thinking about setting one up. It should be soon though, how about with your next product?

A Short Quiz. How Well Do You Analyze the Affiliate Profit Potential of Your Products?

Time for a little break from the figures. Just in case you're a little unclear about what I just said above, I want to hit you with a few examples to demonstrate my point, and to prove that you do actually know how to analyze the situation effectively and make changes to your advantage. So here are some examples, and some questions for you. **You just learned how to do something new. Here's the proof.**

Example one: A year or two back (This is a true story by the way), someone I met through one of my sites tried to strike a joint venture deal with me. It was a JV of the simplest kind. He gives me higher commissions, and I promote his product. Ignoring the quality of the product right now and just concentrating on it's earning potential, he had a $57 product, and offered me two dollars per sale, one off commission. It's probably quite obvious at this point that I said no at the time, and for good reason.

Would you promote anything for $2 per sale on a one off single level commission? There are far better deals out there.

So what do you reckon he could have done to entice me further, improving his offer at the same time? Try and come up with a couple of ideas based on what we've just talked about before reading on.

How about bringing the commissions up to an even 60% for a start? It was a JV after all, so I'd expect higher than average commissions. Even at 50%, I may have been tempted to accept. Hey, it's a quick burst of cash, it was possible I may have said yes. So how else could he have enticed me? Remember back to the four points we discussed a few minutes ago..

How about some commissions over two level? That would have meant my one off promotion, while not reoccurring isn't quite so one off anymore. If he wanted to entice me further, he could have dropped the commissions to maybe 45-50% and offer a monthly recurring commission if the product allowed this.

Taking things a step further, what if the product he had been selling for $57 was a low ticket item that fed through to a high priced one off sale for $200-$2000 per sale at 50% commission? I definitely would have gone ahead then if the product was quality.

Do you see how bad design of a pay plan or product in general can doom it failure from the start, unable to be revived without some major overhauls to how the whole sales system works? You may wonder why you'd change the way your whole business works just to get me promoting, but that's not what it's about. In general, affiliates are after the same thing in a program they're going to promote, whether it's me, or any of the other thousands upon thousands of them out there.

Can you also see how through this last snippet of information about bringing a low priced product through to a high priced product, you can attract people who wouldn't normally promote a $20-$50 product for someone else? There's plenty of people out there who only promote for others if it's a high ticket item. This is a great way to carve your way through the competition and start pulling in the joint venture prospects that do just that. Joint ventures are a whole new ball game however, so we'll continue on now through affiliate management.

All About Adding Value

So you see, it's all about adding value, something that many demote to just a product sales relevant technique, however it is one of the biggest improvements you can make to any of the resource building parts of your business, be it affiliates, list building, JV's, returning customers, any of them. Your product doesn't have to be the most expensive, or offer the highest first level commissions in the world. It doesn't even have to off reoccurring commissions either, but it does have to be worthwhile for anyone to consider promoting for you.

And remember, it's about building affiliates for the future rather than to make a shed load of money in a few hours. If you have to give a little bit more away short term to gain long term affiliates and contacts, that's definitely one heck of a good deal. Don't think of it as having to wait. Think of it as having the choice to earn $100 extra a week for the rest of your life, or having to be patient but earn $1000 and more extra per week for the rest of your life for example. I know which one I'd choose.

The General Rule

Here's a general rule to go by. It doesn't apply in all cases, but in most. The better your product is, and the more the affiliate earns over time, or the higher the commission for the single sale product, the more affiliates you will attract, the more money you'll make. This should give you a good insight into what to do with your levels, reoccurring level, and overall percentage.

If in doubt, pull out that calculator and start working out how much you and your affiliates will earn with a select number of sales over a period of time in a theoretical situation. There's nothing wrong with doing this to get an idea of the kind of figures you're likely to be seeing, but I'll be honest with you, nothing beats testing, not to mention playing with numbers is a heck of a good motivator.

A Brief Glance at Innovations

One more thing we need to look at when we are dealing with what kind of percentages to give your affiliates and what levels to set these at. There are some innovative ideas floating around out there about getting the most out your affiliates with regards to commissions. Look at quick start bonuses for example. How about offering 100% commissions for the first month, and then a smaller percentage ongoing afterwards? Quick start bonuses seem to be growing ever popular in the race to have affiliates promoting your product. It's worth thinking about what other types of ways, bonuses, and loyalty schemes for long term affiliates you can bring to life, too. You just might come up with the next big thing. If you're unsure though, it's best just to go with tried and tested methods we're talking about here.

Ok now we're done with setting up the affiliate program itself, and you know how to go about levels, reoccurring systems and percentages depending on your situation, it's time to look at those all important methods of actually getting these affiliates that have signed up to promote for you effectively. Not just once, but over and over again, because let's face it; An army of loyal affiliates means you can keep churning out quality products, and you've got people there ready to promote for you, and that's before you've sent ads to your list, anyone else's or gone in search of joint ventures for the project. Powerful stuff.

We'll do this after a quick summary of what we've just talked about so it's easier to commit to memory. Skip the summary if you don't need a refresher or believe all the information has sufficiently sunk in up to this point.

Affiliate Program Management Summary

• What you won't find here is technical information. What you will find is solid marketing information that's going to make sure that you get the best out of your affiliates, and to demonstrate why this should be one of your highest priorities.

• Let's talk first about affiliate programs and how important they are, and what they'll do for your business. Also how they have a correlation, or even a direct connection to another marketing methods that we'll talk about in a moment.

• So, why do affiliate programs make success much easier to come by? Well, to put it as bluntly as I can, can you imagine trying to sell a thousand units of your product on your own? That'd be pretty harsh on your pocket, and your time in most cases.

- Now, imagine you had a hundred people standing beside you with the same or greater promotion power than you. Can you imagine selling a thousand units of your product now you have a hundred helpers? You've immediately multiplied your promotion power by one hundred times.
- Let me put a scene to you using real monetary terms. You've just launched a brand new product, which happens to be pretty similar to someone you know, Mr. X. You both launch at the same time, but the difference is you've taken affiliate marketing seriously and have 150 affiliates in your system already, where he has none.

- Both of your products are priced at $500, and you both each manage to sell ten products, totally on your own, for a profit of $5000 each. You're about even so far, until your affiliates come in. Of course not all your affiliates are going to be heavy hitters or even promote anything, but lets say for this example, just a measly 10% of them make three sales each in that same month at 60% commissions.

- Pulling out my handy calculator, I can tell you that those small number of sales have just made you an additional $9000 and $13500 for your affiliates, bringing your total profit for the month to $14000.

- While you and your affiliates are laughing all the way to the bank, Mr. X is devastated because he didn't put an affiliate system into action and pull in the type of money and success that you have.

- Now, you can see the importance of such systems. Don't let anyone ever tell you that you're wasting your time setting this up, or attracting affiliates. You'll likely hear things like 'I tried it but hardly any affiliates promoted for me'. You can see how few it takes to really make your earnings something special.

- It's true that the rates of promotion can vary, depending on your business, and the quality and experience of the affiliates. Some will forget they signed up. Some will sign up and then get distracted, and some just haven't built up the resources to point that they can readily make many sales. We'll address this in a moment.

- Looking at this type of sales figure always gets me excited. Have you ever seen people making 40, 50, 60 even a hundred thousand dollars plus per month, and wondered how they pull in this amount? Well, let me tell you, affiliates are a big part of it in most cases. Don't miss out, or you might find yourself just getting by instead of extremely comfortable where income is concerned.

- The second reason that you may be told affiliate promotion isn't worth it is the notion that affiliates are hard to find. This goes in the same box as list building. It's not hard to do if you know how.

- We're going to jump ahead now, and start to build up a picture of the ideal affiliate program, with a view to getting your affiliates promoting. The rest of this report contains some fundamentals, so keep reading even if you don't have a system set up yet because it will provide a solid knowledge base and assist you in understanding what your software needs to be capable of.

- First and foremost, a big aspect in getting affiliates in the first place and getting them to promote for you is the front line, the commission per sale that you're offering them. Think high.

- I want you to put it out of your mind that giving affiliates more per sale than you make yourself is a bad thing and you're losing money, because you're definitely not.

- Lets look at some examples to show you that high commissions on paper looks like less profit for you, but in practice actually means more profit for you. A short term single sale and a long term recurring membership commission example.

- Lets start with the membership site. Let's imagine that you're running a membership site with a price tag of $15 per month. Within a single month, if you managed to refer 200 members on your own, that's $3000 per month. Not bad, a handy little earner. The problem comes when you start talking 60% commissions for affiliates. That leaves you with $6 per month profit per sale. Doesn't sound a lot does it?

- That looks like a massive cut in profits, but lets say again that you have 150 affiliates, and this time, due to the lower price, and it being slightly easier to get people to part with their cash compared to a $500 product, 15 of your affiliates refer 15 members each that just happen to stay with you for a year. That's a miniscule $300 extra per week. Now some might see that as not worth it, but let's add that up, $16,200 per year. It looks a better now. I could buy myself a juicy 64" plasma screen or 6 brand new top of the range computers. What would you spend an extra $16k on? Not a bad little earner for something that originally took your profit per sale down to a measly $6, especially when you take these very modest figures and spread them over several products.

• I think this is where the whole affiliate program is a bad thing and cut profits state of mind comes in, but that's not the case. A sale by an affiliate earning 60% doesn't cut your profits by 60%, instead it's a gain of 40% on a sale you may not have made in the first place. This is my personal reasoning for not being worried about setting higher than average commissions (60% and upwards). The potential for this is huge.

• The one thing that I do want to show you right away, before we start talking about response rates and the like, is that building affiliates is not an overnight thing. It's like list building, the more products you launch, and promote, the more Jv's will come your way, and in turn the more people will join your list and your affiliate program. Don't fret though, just because it won't happen overnight, you'll see later, that it can take just a few weeks.

• Let's look at some of the nuances an specifics of actually running your affiliate program now, beginning with the forefront of your affiliate system, your commissions.

• Your first option when setting up your system,

will likely be how much do I grant in commissions and on how many levels? The answer in itself really isn't all as complex as it might seem.

• The first thing you need to do is look at things from an affiliate's point of view. We've been spoiled lately with commissions as high as 80/90 even a hundred percent for single month in quick start bonuses.

• Taking this into account, your commissions on the first level should be at the absolute bare minimum 40%. Anything less and you won't attract the numbers or the quality in your affiliates. You should think of 50-55%% as an average nowadays with anything above that, above average.

• Next up, level two. The all important second level, an important aspect from your affiliates point of view, due to this providing them with a reoccurring passive income, where the people they refer, refer others, and they earn on this.

• I know people who won't even promote affiliate programs unless they have a second level up there (very important to keep this in mind), so a second level commissions is a must. Use your discretion, and remember whilst you're selecting your levels and commissions to look at things as if you were promoting your stuff as an affiliate. If it doesn't look like an attractive deal to you, it probably won't to anyone else either, and you need to improve that before launching.

• There can, however, be times when 40% commissions and a second level commission may not be viable for tangible products for example, or if you have high per product production costs.

- Still, in this case, go ahead and create yourself an affiliate program, whether it's five, ten or even twenty percent. It may not get you as much interest and your affiliates might not come in as thick and as fast, but you're still making additional sales, albeit at a slower pace.

- The next thing we need to look at when setting affiliate commissions is your product price and your product structure. There are four situations and product types that really pull in the performing affiliates. These four conditions are: one, where you have a high ticket item, two when you've set higher than average commissions and three, when the commissions are reoccurring over time, whether it's a direct reoccurrence of a monthly membership site, or an indirect reoccurrence of a second level, four providing a passive income for the affiliates promoting.

- I've had people ask me why they're having trouble attracting affiliates that actually promote something for them, and more often than not, their product is a $10 one off sale with no follow-up product. $5 one off commissions isn't going to attract anyone. Would you promote this product when you have a choice of using your hard earned resources and promoting for 60, 70 even eighty percent commissions, either reoccurring or on products from $60 up to $1500?

- So before you actually decide to shell out on some sort of affiliate system, make sure that you don't price yourself too high, offer commissions that are too low, non-recurring or don't have a second level. **Put yourself in the affiliates' shoes.**

- Just to give you an example of the kind of offers you're going to start to receive when word gets out, the very first offer I received was from someone promoting a $57 product that offered me $2 per sale. When I told him I don't even consider promoting for anything less than 40% he was shocked that he'd have to give so much away as he put it.

- So, what do you reckon he could have done to entice me further? How about bringing the commissions up to an even 60% for a start? It was a JV after all, so I'd expect higher than average commissions. I may have even been tempted to accept 50%. Hey, it's a quick burst of cash. It was possible I may have said yes. So how else could he have enticed me? How about some commissions over two levels? That would have meant my one off promotion, while not reoccurring isn't quite so one off anymore. If he wanted to entice me further, he could have dropped the commissions to maybe 45-50% and offered a monthly recurring commission. Taking things a step further, what if the product he had been selling for $57 was a low ticket item that fed through to a high priced one off sale for $500-$2000 per sale at 50% commissions? I definitely would have gone ahead then if the product was quality.

- So, you see, your product doesn't have to be the most expensive or have the highest commissions. It doesn't even have to be reoccurring, but you must make it worth while from the affiliate's point of view.

- Here's a general rule to go by. It doesn't apply in all cases, but in most. The better your product is, and the more the affiliate earns over time, or the higher the commission for the single sale product, the more affiliates you will attract, the more money you'll make.

- This should give you a good insight into what to do with your levels, reoccurring level, and overall percentage. If in doubt, pull out that calculator and start working out how much you and your affiliates will earn with a select number of sales, over a period of time in a theoretical situation. There's nothing wrong with doing this to get an idea of the kind of figures you're likely to be seeing, but I'll be honest with you, nothing beats testing.

- Now, one more thing to look at when we're dealing with what kind of percentage to give your affiliates and what levels to set these at. There are some innovative ideas floating around out there about getting the most out your affiliates with regards to commissions. Look at quick start bonuses for example. How about offering 100% commissions for the first month, and then a smaller percentage ongoing afterwards? Quick start bonuses seem to be growing ever popular in the race to have affiliates promoting your product. It's worth thinking about what other ways, bonuses, and loyalty schemes for long term affiliates, too. You just might come up with the next big thing. If you're unsure though, it's best just to go with tried and tested methods being discussed here.

- Ok now we're done with setting up the affiliate program itself, and you know how to go about levels, reoccurring systems and percentages depending on your situation. It's time to look at those all important methods of actually getting these affiliates that have signed up to promote for you effectively. Not just once, but over and over again. An army of loyal affiliates making both them and you a lot of money.

Overview of Affiliate Management — Part 2

• To show you the number one mistake many marketers make when they're creating their own products and running their own affiliate program.

• To introduce the concept of linking your affiliate system to other resources, such as your list, joint ventures, and your previous customers.

• To demonstrate how dead ends occur all over unfinished marketing sites, and these people are losing affiliates, money and customers. Lets plug those dead ends right now.

• To help see things from the affiliates point of view. Your affiliate system needs to be quick, snappy, and instant, not long and complicated.

• To show you how to provide your affiliates with everything they need to promote, removing the problem of distractions and 'I'll promote this later' syndromes.

• To help you understand how to keep your current affiliates flowing, and how they're going to pull you in a bundle of cash over multiple products over many years.
• To show you how to treat your affiliates, and how not to treat them with regards to future contact and advertising. Something which if done incorrectly will lose you everyone who's previously been promoting your stuff. Not good.

• To show that no matter how slow the growth when you first start attracting affiliates, it is exponential and will snowball real fast, but only if you let it.

Affiliate Program Management - Part 2

Ok, so we've had a good look at aspects relating to the selection of percentages, levels, and whether or not to run an affiliate program. Right now, we're going to jump ahead a little bit, and start talking about how to actually manage those affiliates once you have them. The most important factors that we're going to address will be related to keeping your affiliates promoting, keeping them loyal, promotion spurts using offers, and at the same time, take a look at some of the biggest mistakes I still see people making every day whilst running their affiliate program.

Big Mistake Number One – Recycling

First up, let's look at how many people manage their affiliates. Here's the situation that I come across most. Person A sets up their website, their product and sales system, and integrates an affiliate program. They go ahead, launch the product, and have their affiliates promote for them. That's all very well, in fact there's nothing wrong with this until you consider what happens when this person goes on and creates a second product.

What you'll likely see is they'll create the product, put up the sales letter and sales system and go about things the same way as they did with their first product. The problem is many marketers don't seem to utilize the affiliates they gathered through the previous product in the promotion of their new product. What a waste. All that promotion and affiliate gathering, and you're just going to throw it all away by starting all over again when you come up with your next product. People say to me, well that's common sense. Sure, but how many are actually doing it?

This is definitely a big no, no. For affiliates being such a great part of online marketing, if you do have several products, you'll want to remember all your affiliates. I wouldn't expect you to get a list of subscribers from one website, then throw them aside and not mail them when your next site launches. The same goes for affiliates. Utilize this powerful tool. There's several ways of doing this of course, you may want to send a mail to your affiliates and let them know about this new promotion opportunity. Your best bet however is to keep all affiliates in the one system for all your websites, and hit them with introductory offers every single time you launch a new product.

Now I know some of you may not have the budget or software to do this, and if you're doing it manually it can take some time. If you're running affiliate promotions though, you'll need to figure out a way of doing this effectively, even if it's just a manual import of all previous affiliates into a second affiliate system, and a mailing that tells them their account is already open, and ready to go, along with an ad they can use, complete with their promotion URL to get them started immediately.

Whilst we're talking about this in fact, I'll let you in

on a little something.

Big Mistake 2 - Dead Ends

Next up, we're going to look at the final part of the actual set up of the affiliate program. It's something that's really important and fundamental in online business, not just for affiliate programs, and that's to link it up, and give your customers a path to follow. Ok that might sound amateurish and maybe a little patronizing, so my apologies for that, however the other day I was browsing around checking out the competition and what they're up to related to my next product, and what I found was many of them, both in their sales letter (if there was one) and in their affiliate signup pages, they dead ended me.

What I mean by that is, I go to sign up for their affiliate program, and they have this great sales page that tells me how much I'm going to earn per sale, a really nice bonus scheme for top affiliates etc, and I got to the bottom of the page, and guess what I found? Well, not much actually. They sold me on this affiliate program, but the page just ended. No click here to sign up, no nothing.

Now that's an extreme example I have to admit, but lets be honest here, if you're seriously getting into affiliate marketing you can't afford to do that. If you have an affiliate's button that leads to a page that explains a little about your affiliate program, try to fit the form in at the base of the page, or at least have a click here to sign up. Granted, normally I wouldn't have mentioned this, but looking around it's definitely worth it. So never forget, a nav bar is good, but you have to show the customer where to go, with click here's, or forms that tell the story for themselves. You're still selling yourself here, and getting the all-important affiliates can be more profitable than making the sale yourself. Don't overlook small things such as this, pick through your setup with a fine toothcomb and make sure no page has a dead end anywhere.

Sell It Like A Product

Still concentrating on the selling aspect of getting your affiliates, we need to plug some more gaps. Mistakes, mistakes everywhere, it's not easy to sign up for some affiliate programs even if you wanted to. Don't be one of those people. They're losing thousands and they probably don't even know it. So here's another little tip for you. Sell your affiliate program.

If I click on your "Affiliates" button on your website, I don't want to be presented with a form that asks for my details. I see this all too often. Write a mini sales letter that explains some things to the potential affiliate. Information you must include can be as basic as how much they'll earn on how many levels, and for how long, and any bonuses they may get for a particular amount of sales in any given time, and of course, how often you pay out.

Once you've got the basics down you can start getting a little more complex and bringing out your tracking figures if you have any. I d be happy about an affiliate program that pays me $500 per sale, but I'd be even happier with an affiliate program that pays me $500 per sale when the sales letter has been proven to have a targeted click through to sales ratio. It's like the creation of your sales letters. Eliminate risk, and build confidence in your product, only this time around, your affiliate program is your product.

Don't Hide It

On a similar note, one more little tip I'd like to give you before moving on is to not hide any information in terms and conditions. Sure put up a terms and conditions, but don't small print any of the important information and leave it out of your sales letter. After all, these people signing up to your affiliate program aren't people you want to annoy in any way. They're going to provide a good chunk of the backbone of your business in the future. Again, like your list, and like your previous customers who will buy from you again and again, these affiliates are at least as important as looking after them. Ok moving on now.

Get Them Promoting

Our next most important factor, and that's what to do with your affiliates once you have some in the system as a result of your product promotion, joint ventures and a well linked site (which we talked about above). So we have our affiliates, we've given the relevant information already, we've got them to sign up, so what's next? Getting them promoting, and keeping them promoting is what we need to get sorted.

Now there's a lot of methods that can be used to both get affiliate promoting and keep them promoting. The problem is when deciding what's going to be appropriate is that you can't only do one of them. There are generally two types of affiliates, the ones who know how to sell and are going to make you money and the ones who don't know how to sell and aren't going to make you money. It sounds harsh, but that pretty much sums it up.

Educate Those That Don't Have a Clue

So the first thing we should be looking at is educating those affiliates that don't know what they're doing, something that the people talking about low sales figures from affiliates overlook. There's plenty of ways to do this, for example, producing your own mini-guide for them, or giving away a small training course. If you're really stuck you could always get your hands on a mini e-book, but if you're going to go down that road, please make sure that it actually makes sense, and wasn't published in 1981. Education is a good way to go, because these people who come into your affiliate program, if they make their first good amount of cash with you, they're going to love you for it, and most likely promote for you again in the future, especially if it's your guide that taught them how to do so.

Promote When You Need Them To Promote

Next along the line you want to be thinking about little tricks, offers and promotions you can run to have your affiliates promoting for you at a particular time. There's nothing more powerful than an army of affiliates by your side ready to promote for you, except that is, an army of affiliates by your side, ready to promote for you, that know how to promote and do so when you most want them to.

Look at things like seasonal bonuses. An extra percentage push near Christmas time is always a good performer, despite the lower visit to sales ratios in the holiday season. Remember we mentioned we're not just after sales here? It doesn't even have to be a special occasion. If you need more cash quickly you can always set a deadline for a month or so down the road, and offer a big bonus to the top performing affiliates or affiliates. In fact this is something that worked real well back at my old site, and was probably one of the very first affiliate offers I put out early in my online marketing career.

I offered the first affiliate to reach 50 sales a $750 bonus on top of their monthly earnings, and they seriously went for this. I had all sorts of traffic coming in from all over the place. Now be careful with this. Don't go offering $5000 at the end of the month to your top affiliate if you've never tested this before. What we don't want to happen is you having to pay 5k out to your top affiliate who was the only one to make any sales. Go about this in a smart way, and set a hard target on the number of sales or amount of earnings needed from an affiliate to earn the additional winnings. This way at least you know how much you'll be making with a particular amount of sales and won't make any big losses, or any losses at all for that matter.

Test It Out & Have a Play – You'll Be Surprised

What I will say to you is test things out, and have a play around. Carefully though, we don't want any unexpected losses to creep up uninvited. Test out different percentages at different periods in the year. Test out big start up bonuses and a large addition to month one commissions if you have a low ticket membership site. What we're looking to get is the most amount of affiliates promoting for you, whilst spending the least. I would love to tell you what works best all the time, however it varies from product to product, business to business, and of course totally depends on your affiliates, how good they are at promotion, and whether they signed up to promote you or just to get the freebie.

One thing I will say though is this. No matter how much extra work this seems, or how little returns it gives over a small number of people, remember, that the numbers in your affiliate system will grow over time. When it does grow, it's going to be your job to make sure you keep on top of the affiliates and keep them promoting. Education and special offers is the way to start.

Quick Start Bonuses Explained

Something else you may want to think about is quick start bonuses. We mentioned these earlier but I never really told you why they're important. Well, it's for two reasons. For a start it provides a viable option for your affiliates and makes your program more enticing for them to join. Hey, who wouldn't join an affiliate program that advertised 100% commissions for the first month or two? I know a few people who went ahead and did this, and they got one heck of a response. Remember always to put yourself in the shoes of your target. Think like them, and you'll be able to attract them.

The second reason for big quick start bonuses is to actually get people promoting. It's amazing sometimes how hard it is to get people to do things. You know how you try your best to get someone to do something or do a job well, and in the end you end up saying something like 'Ah I'll just do it myself'. Well this is the job of quick start bonuses on a deeper level. If you're attracting affiliates that generally don't promote very often or haven't promoted before, then this is another reason for them to choose you. Once they're going and start to make money, it's amazing how much of a motivation enhancement it is to receive an e-mail saying you've just made some cash. Quick start bonuses are especially important when you have a membership site that doesn't cost a huge amount per month, but you can take advantage of a big and powerful high commission headline to attract them. Don't forget all of this is tied to you and your business also, important for repeat affiliate business. If someone gives you cash, you don't forget it, and no doubt you'll be back for more, as will your affiliates flood back to you over multiple businesses.

Communication – The Key to Profits

Which brings me to my final point, and probably the most important one in this section. Communication is the key. As well as sending bonuses and offers, an e-mail with a 'Congrats, you've made cash' subject can be one heck of a motivator. It's also important to remind your affiliates, not necessarily through offers, but often letting them in on info like 'It can take seven times and upwards of 10 times that people have to see your offer before they will sign up'.

We've seen those before, and that is the purpose. I have found to an extent that with mailing list advertising, this is indeed true, provides a good excuse for you to mail your affiliates, and also provides them with the confidence they need to know that send out another mailing to their list isn't going to be a waste of time. They'll gobble up any free info and tips you can give them, simply because it means more money for them. (And for you in this case).

Crafting Your Welcome & Congrats E-mails

Make sure you craft your congratulations e-mails and welcome emails well. Still on the subject of mailing your affiliates, it's important for everything to be smooth, quick and easy for them. Some just have lists that they want to blast your ads out to. Your job is to make that as smooth as possible. Send them a log in link in the welcome mail, tell them again how much they'll earn, give them some small stats and figures; 'With just '10 sales, you'll earn $7000'. Emphasize the second levels, no matter how small. This passive earning is really important to a lot of marketers.

Think of this as kind of a small sales letter, but crossed with an instruction manual. They've signed up, now sell onto the promotion with how much they can earn and how quickly. Don't forget to tell them to click the link below, copy and paste the pre-written ads, blast them out to their lists or the list of provided e-zines, and await the congratulatory e-mails from you, saying they have cash. Don't just suggest an action and expect them to do it. Close the sale. Tell them to do it, and your response will increase dramatically.

Emphasize pay days, and tell them to look out for special promotions and bonuses from you that will give them the opportunity to promote your other products, or even promote this product at a higher commission. This really should have gone in the bonuses section that we talked about earlier, but since we're here, try not to give the reader any excuse to hold off.

For example, I remember four years or so back I joined a membership site and was all ready to go off promoting for them as an affiliate, then when I saw the welcome mail, I was told to look forward to an e-mail soon that would entitle me to extra earnings promoting the product. Just that wording almost put me off. I later found out that it was actually bonuses and top affiliate rewards for the previous couple of months, but see how that mail seemed like a good deal, but made me wait? No doubt this was the opposite effect they were looking for.

You don't want your affiliates to think twice. This letter will have them log in, grab the ad and blast it out. As quick and as easy as possible for them with the best possible rewards, which in turn means the highest amount of additional income for you. Give it a try. You won't be disappointed.

Don't Mistreat Your Affiliates

This also brings up an even more important point that I see a heck of a lot. Ever had this? You join an affiliate program, do a little promotion, receive your cash, and before long you're receiving ads because the persons affiliate program added you to an all out advert list that they're charging to send to? Granted it's not so bad if you know the person, have bought or expressed interest in the products they happen to be selling, but I'll be honest with you, if you just add affiliates to a mailing list, you're missing out big time.

They're going to get annoyed at getting something they didn't sign up for, and if just one good affiliate un-subscribes... I'll leave that to you to figure out exactly how much money that could mean you lose in the coming months or with the launch of your next product.

Some people don't agree with me here, I have to admit. But the general rule is, if your affiliates really are valuable (which they should be) and have been promoting for you, don't send them adverts for anything. The only exception is for a special offer for the affiliate program, notification of a new product they can promote, or something of that sort. Like your list, and on a smaller but more personal scale your JV prospects. These are not people you want to annoy, because quite frankly, they'll just leave and go elsewhere and you'll lose wads of cash, maybe not today, maybe not tomorrow, but in the future, you will lose long term. Way too many small businesses seem to do this. I wonder if they know what they're doing to their earning prospects.

General rule of thumb here, if they asked for it, send it to them. Marketing is only intrusive and annoying if it's not wanted. If they signed up for something, don't start sending them unrelated information, which will only annoy them and lose you money. This doesn't just relate to affiliate programs either, this goes for mailing lists, newsletters, e-zines, personal lists and more than anything, especially joint venture prospects.

A Final Word

I'm glad we got that one covered here in the time that we have, because it really is as important as I keep saying. In fact, in case I still haven't managed to convince you, I want to finish with one more example of a high ticket item. Let's say you've created a guide, on a subject you find interesting, and sold it for $1000 including audio, video, consultations, and DVDs. You make fifteen sales from joint ventures yourself in the first month, and make $15,000. Now with 150 affiliates, just ten percent of them making two sales each at 50% commissions. You've just netted yourself an extra... I'll let you do the math on that one so it really sinks in how powerful this is and gets the juices flowing.

Alright, before we move off the subject of affiliates

into the other attached manuals, I just want to re-iterate. Affiliate growth is exponential. It's slow at the start, and gets faster, depending on your joint ventures, list size and the number of affiliates you have. Every product, every single piece of software or information you release relating to your business should have this in mind.

Don't worry if when you first start building affiliates they don't quite make you as much as you hoped. This is totally normal. What you'll find is, in every twenty, thirty, fifty, or even 100 affiliates, there are a couple of real gems there that make you (and them) a whole lot of cash. Take it from me, take your affiliate building as seriously as everyone's been telling us to take our list building and direct sales recently, and you'll see some amazing results.

Summary

• Ok, we've had a look previously at some of the statistic based aspects of selecting percentages and commission levels for your affiliate system. You should already have a good idea of what works and what doesn't allowing you to select the right numbers for your business.

• Let's move on now from percentages and look at some important ways to get your affiliates promoting, and keep them promoting while touching on some of the biggest mistakes people make when setting up and managing their affiliates from the start. Lets finish creating a solid foundation for your business.

- First and foremost, something that also applies to list building, something that many marketers do for one reason or another, that's starting again, but this time instead of straight up deleting important resources, they're doing something even worse.

- Here's what you'll see from a lot of marketers out there. They create a product, gather their resources including affiliates, and when they're done and move on to their next product they don't take their affiliates with them.

- Why not? They worked hard to get them, they're just as important as any other resources, if not more important, yet they're throwing them away. Even if your affiliate system doesn't support multiple products and multiple domains, it's a simple case of exporting and importing, and firing out a special higher commission for people who have promoted for you before. There are no excuses for not utilizing this powerful tool, after all, we've already talked about how the hardest and most expensive part of marketing is getting new customers, new affiliates, and new subscribers. Don't throw them away when you begin to get them. You earned these resources, you deserve to keep them, and keep making money from them, as they make money from your products too.

- Next up, let's move onto a fundamental of business, not just for affiliate programs. That's give your customers a path to follow, and a call to action. I've seen sites that have great sales letters, or great products and at the end of it, when I come to order there's just a dead end. No order link, nothing, and I have on several occasions had to search for the order link, even from well known sites that reach millions every day. Who knows how many sales they're losing by cutting off the customer's path and their flow.

- To begin this flow of affiliates, you need to link to your affiliate program on every page of your site, and when this link is clicked, there should be a sales letter there, not just a signup form. Shorter than the product sales letter, it's still there to persuade people and sell yourself and your products. Without this, you're selling yourself short.

- After this, and most importantly, a call to action. Don't just give them a form, or worse still, leave them with a dead end. Place your signup form or link to sign up after a call to action to do so. Don't let people have to search for anything. Remember what we said heavy hitting affiliates like? Straight in, blast ad, straight out, earn money. It's a simple as that, and the easier and more flowing you make your affiliate signup process, the more affiliates you're going to see signing up.

- Here's an example for you, I go to sign up for an affiliate program, and they have this great sales page that tells me how much I'm going to earn per sale, a really nice bonus scheme for top affiliates etc, and I got to the bottom of the page, and guess what I found? Well, not much actually. They sold me on this affiliate program, but the page just ended. No click here to sign up, no nothing. Ever seen a site like that? Whether it's affiliate programs or sales letters? If you haven't, you can bet you'll start to notice them now.

• This is something that loses marketers literally wads of cash, if you remember back to the difference to your income just fifteen affiliates can make, and you should be able to see how devastating mistakes like this are. Worst of all, they probably don't even know they're doing it. If you want the potential customer or resource to do something, you have to point them to it, giving them a gentle shove in the right direction.

• If I click on your "Affiliates" button on your website, I don't want to be presented with a form that asks for my details. I see this all too often. Write a mini sales letter that explains some things to the potential affiliate. Information you must include can be as basic as how much they'll earn on how many levels, and for how long, and any bonuses they may get for a particular amount of sales in any given time, and of course, how often you pay out. This is what's going to get me (as a an affiliate of yours) promoting for you.

• Another tip, something to do for your own benefit and the affiliates benefit. You'd be surprised at how powerful a signup page for an affiliate system becomes when you've proven the product they're promoting is quality, and that the sales letter selling it has been tried and proven.

• I'd be happy about an affiliate program that pays me $500 per sale, but I'd be even happier with an affiliate program that pays me $500 per sale, when the sales letter has been proven to have a specific click through to sales ratio. It's just like your sales letter writing. Eliminate risk, and build confidence in your product, only this time around, your affiliate program is your product. Never forget you're always selling, this is no different to writing a sales letter for your products.

• On a similar note, of course we're going to need a terms and conditions section in there. Don't hide anything in it. Tell the affiliates the whole story on your sales letter, everything from when payday is to how much they'll earn and how many sales they need to make to get to a certain level of commissions. Keep the terms and conditions for legal stuff, like pointing out you can't guarantee any earnings and you're not responsible for them if they give their details out and the like. You're giving out all the info you can on your sales letter for the affiliate program for the sake of the affiliates not having to search for important information, the time in which between reading, signing up and promoting, the time where they're most likely to be distracted and leave you without their profitable promotion.

• Sharing so much information straight up alone can make you tens of thousands in affiliate sales that you wouldn't have normally received.

• So, we have our affiliates, we've given the relevant information already, we've got them to sign up, so what's next? Getting them promoting, and keeping them promoting is what we need to get sorted.

• There are generally two type of affiliates, the ones that know how to sell and are going to make you money and the ones who don't know how to sell and aren't going to make you money. It sounds harsh, but that pretty much sums it up. Keep this in mind when looking at your affiliate stats. Just because they have ten thousand hits to their affiliate link, doesn't mean they know how to promote, that could have easily come from guaranteed hits and you'll be getting downhearted about nothing, when it's actually the quality of their traffic at fault.

• To solve the problem of those signing up who don't know how to promote yet or don't have the resources is not an easy job, in fact, the only thing you can do to get them to make sales is educate them. Either by producing your own mini-guide or searching for an affiliate promotion guide with re-sell/give away rights, which is always a good investment to make.

• This can take a long time, however, and you won't see results straight away. It all depends on their willingness to learn. You should direct 99% of your attention to those who already know how to promote, and make sure they keep promoting and getting a good deal for both parties over multiple products. That's the only way that you'll be able to run a successful affiliate base.

• Here are some ideas that we put into action and have already tested. First and foremost are bonuses for affiliates. What do you think of when I say bonuses for affiliates? Well you wouldn't be wrong if you have several ideas because there's a lot of leeway here. Our aim is to get them selling and keep them selling resulting in huge profits for you, the way to do this is to make it in their best interests to promote your stuff.

- How about seasonal bonuses, an extra percentage push a few months before Christmas? Look at it like this, we all want more money at Christmas to buy our loved ones those extra special presents or whisk them away for a weekend, and your affiliates want the same, so give them a reason to earn their money from your products.

- Bigger bonuses for the whole month, bigger bonuses for top performing affiliates for example. In fact this was one of the things that filled my original site with members.

- I offered the first affiliate to reach 50 sales a $750 bonus on top of their monthly earnings, and everyone went for it. I had all sorts of traffic coming in from all over the place. Now be careful with this. Don't go offering $5000 at the end of the month to your top affiliate if you've never tested this before. What we don't want to happen is you having to pay 5k out to your top affiliate who was the only one to make any sales. Go about this in a smart way, and set a hard target on the number of sales or amount of earnings needed from an affiliate to earn the additional winnings. This way at least you know how much you'll be making with a particular amount of sales and won't make any big losses or any losses at all.

- Now I know this might seem a little bit of extra work, and depending on your affiliate software, it can indeed be a hassle, however, trust me when I say it's worth it. It's not the difference between making an extra sale here, it's the difference between getting affiliates promoting who otherwise wouldn't, or have stopped and moved on resulting in who knows how many sales. Five, ten, a hundred, thousands, even tens of thousands of dollars are at your disposal. Let's make sure we use this.

- Quick start bonuses also work real well. First it provides a viable option for your affiliates if your site has a low price (for example, a $27 membership site may offer 100% for the first one or two months in commissions before moving onto the regular two level 50/15 commissions). Who wouldn't join an affiliate program that offers 100% commissions? That's one heck of a powerful thing to be able to say about your affiliate program.

- Second, it actually gets people promoting. It's amazing sometimes how hard it is to get people to do things. You know how you try your best to get someone to do something or do a job well, and in the end you end up saying something like 'Ah I'll just do it myself'. Well this is the job of quick start bonuses on a deeper level. If you're attracting affiliates that generally don't promote very often or haven't promoted before, then this is another reason for them to choose you.

- The next tip. Send congratulatory e-mails. Your software should do this for you as standard and it's one heck of a motivator. Pack in quick and easy links to the affiliate system and your ads. It never gets old seeing 'You've got Cash!' or 'Congrats, you made a sale!' as a subject line.

• This is really important, so make sure you craft your congratulations e-mails and welcome emails well. Everything should be quick and easy for affiliates. Some just have lists that they want to blast your ads out to. Your job is to make that as smooth as possible. Send them a log in link in the welcome mail, tell them again how much they'll earn, give them some small stats and figures, "With just 10 sales, you'll earn $700C". Emphasize the second levels, no matter how small. This passive earning is really important to a lot of marketers.

• I remember about four years back I joined a membership site and was all ready to go off promoting for them as an affiliate, then when I saw the welcome mail, I was told to look forward to an e-mail soon that would entitle me to extra earnings promoting the product. Just that wording almost put me off. I later found out that it was actually bonuses and top affiliate rewards for the previous couple of months, but see how that made me wait? You don't want your affiliates to think twice. This letter will have them log in, grab the ad and blast it out. As quick and as easy as possible for them, with the best possible rewards, means and the highest amount of additional income for you. Give it a try. You won't be disappointed.

• This also brings up an even more important point that I see a heck of a lot. Ever had this? You join an affiliate program, do a little promotion, receive your cash or whatever, and before long you're receiving ads because the persons affiliate program added you to an all out advert list that they're charging to send to. Way to go annoying affiliates. I have to admit, some people don't agree with me here, but as far as I'm concerned, every affiliate is valuable and should not be bombarded by ads to buy your stuff. They're there to make money through promotion, not receive ads about your brand new piece of software. Understanding the role of each of your resources is important.

No ads, just offers that relate to the one thing they've already told you and show you that they're good at, and interested in doing, making a whole bunch of cash for themselves and for you.

- Let's say you've created a guide, and sold it for $1000, including audio, video, a free consultation and some DVDs. You make fifteen sales from joint ventures yourself in the first month, and make $15,000. Now with 150 affiliates, with just ten percent of them making two sales each at 50% commissions, you've just netted yourself an extra... I'll let you do the math on that one so it really sinks in how powerful this is.

- Affiliate growth is exponential. It's slow at the start, and gets faster, depending on your joint ventures, list size and the number of affiliates you have. Every product, every single piece of software or information you release relating to your business should have this in mind.

- Don't worry if when you first start building affiliates they don't quite make you as much as you hoped. This is totally normal. What you'll find is, in every twenty, thirty, fifty, or even 100 affiliates, there are a couple of real gems there that make you (and them) a whole lot of cash. Take it from me, take your affiliate building as seriously as everyone's been telling us to take our list building recently, and you'll see some amazing results.

ABOUT THE AUTHOR

Chris Lutz is the founder and owner of **S.P.A.R.T.A.** With more than a decade of professional experience and a business owner, his business now provides other business owners with tools and resources to run more professional and organized operations.

Chris owns and consults for other businesses in all industries currently and is the author of several other books –

The Entrepreneur Lifestyle
Start, Operate, and Grow Your Personal Training Business
Metabolic Resistance Training
Maximum Fat Loss, Minimum Time
Is Your Healthy Diet Making You Fat? Why You Can't Seem to Lose Fat No Matter What You Do.

His website, www.theentrepreneurlifestyle.com is a celebration of the lifestyle of entrepreneurs and teaches them how to go from struggle to success with tools, eCourses, and other resources for entrepreneurs.

Chris' other website, www.lutzlures.com is an ecommerce site for the outdoor enthusiast and, specifically kayak fishermen.